After Dark

DAVID HARSENT

After Dark

LONDON
OXFORD UNIVERSITY PRESS
NEW YORK   TORONTO
1973

Oxford University Press, Ely House, London W.1

GLASGOW NEW YORK TORONTO MELBOURNE WELLINGTON
CAPE TOWN IBADAN NAIROBI DAR ES SALAAM LUSAKA ADDIS ABABA
DELHI BOMBAY CALCUTTA MADRAS KARACHI LAHORE DACCA
KUALA LUMPUR SINGAPORE HONG KONG TOKYO

ISBN 0 19 211834 X

*Printed in Great Britain by
The Bowering Press Limited Plymouth*

To my father

ACKNOWLEDGEMENTS

A NUMBER of these poems have previously appeared in the following publications: *Agenda*, *Antaeus* (USA), the *New York Times*, *New Statesman*, *London Magazine*, *New Poems 1971–2* and *New Poems 1972–3*: P. E. N. anthologies (Hutchinson), *The Times Literary Supplement*, the *Poetry Book Society Supplement*, and the *Review*. *Two Postscripts to My Father* and *Ashridge* appeared as a Sycamore Broadsheet.

I am grateful to the Arts Council of Great Britain for financial assistance given during 1970–71.

D.H.

CONTENTS

vii

Two Postscripts to my Father

As you approached the farmhouse, came
the roar and sudden heat
and the moment when everything paused as you fell,
acres of sky
revolving and sliding away;
then you struck.
The world, you said,
shrank to a splash of blood as the pain began.

Your young wife, the child you'd never seen,
that cold house on the moor's edge:
how could you begin
to piece it all together. . . . On the way
back to the field ambulance, you cried
feeling the steel
slivers bite inside your wounded head.

2

For twenty-five years
you kept those secrets. Dragged yourself
home from icy scaffoldings and plunged
pinched hands into the hollow of the grate,
or stumbled through the leavings of a dream
at three or four or five o'clock,
to thrust your head beneath
a gushing tap, wanting to soak
the pain away. And all the time
love beat like some mad bird against
the bars beneath your skull.

Now it is late October and the high winds have begun—
streaming through the stand of elms beyond my gate,
putting entire hillsides on the move.
Those early photographs litter my desk.
Smiling, sunburned, young, you lounge
against a thirty-pounder
or, hands on hips, stare straight
out at me. There's no way back
through all that violence. We live
seven miles apart and seldom meet.

After Dark

Strange that I should think of them so much,
those journeys he undertook: all those renewals.

I have bogged down in this odd village;
my children belong to the place.
At night I can hear the cows
coughing in a field behind the house.

I close my eyes
and invent arrivals.

Plant

As the train slowed I could see the plant
glimmering in its own steam,
a tangle of pipes and fragile catwalks.

He watched it too, as he told me again
how he saw Italy for the first time
and Africa, like a graveyard.

Old Photographs

The women are dark and seem
very beautiful; the men
look nervous, overdressed.
It's always summer, where they stand,
arms linked, facing the sun,
their blurred smiles meant for no one.

The Turn of the Century

High summer in the southern counties.
Beyond the french windows
two black labradors sprawled on the sloping lawn,
and children splashed
in the stream where the garden ended.

She placed a wicker chair back in the shade
(the lace of her peignoir falling across her throat)
and began the letter.
                    'Dear Mama,
Charles bought me a bonnet when he went
to Bristol last,
and Mary-Ann trimmed it . . .'

White, trailing hands;
a tiny plume
of red staining her handkerchief.

Myth

His first clear memory:
the sky dull red at midnight,
a semi-circle pulsing into black,
and massive winds
roaring across the marshland.

The house was proof
against those far disasters.
Each night, in his mother's bed,
he watched the shadows looming on the wall,
a slow procession of defeated heroes.

Homecoming

A sense of history
unadorned, like algebra,
the main road empty at noon,
a clock
ticking by the fragrant stairwell.
And I am here,
a tourist in other people's lives.

My childhood
must be somebody's dark secret.

Rorschach

A moth is fluttering behind my eyes,
cool blue membrane of wings

lighting the iris
where the sights thread through.

A weir beside a road,
a granite gateway, orchards, and beyond

mile after mile of moorland,
then the sea.

This one is the house; the walled garden,
two figures, cowled.

Pictures of dreams
blurred by blue mothlight.

Those endless grasslands
no one walks but me,

scoured coastlines, towers of rock,
that house;

the pitiless revisions,
the unquenchable white silences.

Encounter

It was a bad day for fishing; it really was;
but the sun flashed tinsel on the wave tops
and the breeze offshore was flattering.
Then, just before lunch,
the power boats rounded the point—
in the foremost prow, the image of his mother.
'Impossible' he muttered, but there she was,
lipstick, eyebrows, hair, her flowered frock,
just like in all the family snapshots.

Cockade

The silence of auditoria, the groan
of ropes on a midnight jetty.

In the stalls, a glove, or a black cockade;
triplets of backwash ticking against the boats.

These are the missing moments in our lives:
perfect, unenjoyed.

Ashridge
In Memoriam B.H.

The light begins to fade; within the wood
the rhythm shifts: from flurries of

songbirds, from startled rabbits
to the smooth, assured

violence of predators. Night-walks
along these tangled paths locked that

rhythm in your head. I think of you
moving among the dark

boles and screens of fern
with your torch, nursing

your fear along—the animals
under cover

circling ceaselessly:
hunter, hunted, hunter. It was years ago.

A wind floats threads of rain
along the shoulder of the hill, where trees

thin down to clumps of bramble.
Four miles away, the village lights

flicker on. I spend most nights indoors,
curled up like some small wintering

animal, amid
my furniture, my rows of unread books.

12

Figures in a Landscape

1

You turn first to the pile of dampish letters:
your love of surprises!
A fall of soot
gives the room its sour smell.

Your disappointment shows.
As you unpack
I watch our farmer-neighbour
herd pigs into a dropside truck.

Slow-witted, dowdy in tweeds and wellingtons,
he cracks his stick
across a straggler's flank
and shambles through the barnyard mud.

2

Once more, evening brings this bright
band of aquamarine above a dim horizon.
Flat, brittle as eggshells.
Then it fades.

Children's toys
rust in our wrecked garden.
Inside the house you cook and keep your peace.
Dulled by steam, your shape passes the window.

3

The car drifts sideways, prodded by the wind.
Pulling it back, I swing the wheel and head
towards the range of hills,
three miles distant, where the wind is massing.

I know the house will show a single light:
the bedroom, where you lie awake
as always, solemn, tranquillized,
wondering if I am on the way.

4

All day the gliders have been drifting overhead;
noiseless, but always there.
Now they sweep in low, circling.

Our children rush
through long grass towards the landing place.
We stand and watch them go.

5

Too tired for sleep and knowing of no way
to quieten you, I've walked to this cold bench.

Above the fields
mountains of purple cloud lumber through drizzle.

Between your open window and this place
the land is dark and wringing wet.

Ski Lift

It was like getting through bad flak,
the wide, blank planes of blue unreachable,
his lungs scorched by the thinning air.

Foothills and a fringe of spruce diminished.
The hotel misted over.
In the lounge, down there, he'd watched the bayonetings.

A month away, and still his mail got through.
The news was always good.
It left him cold, or feeble with regret.

Out of touch was best,
his gloves iced to the bar that locked him in,
the cable hissing overhead.

Choughs tumbled into view like smuts in steam
as he reached the topmost pylon.
His chair rumbled across.

He'd spend his days on those fast slopes below
and sleep the rest.
He was tired of seeing the blood run.

Here

It is grey rain
and you moving about these cold rooms
like an exile.

Morning comes
with a flurry of wings
outside the window. Wake up;

the valley is coddled in mist
as before. Wake up,
you can begin your vigil,

waiting for the dim
stars to reappear,
for the wind to sharpen,

for the last
slow flocks of birds above
this ragged skyline.

Terms

The place put you at risk.
Stone buildings and a few bleak clumps of birch
ranged out along the low escarpments.
The house was still your territory though.
For a while, I thought you'd be content
idling amid your gimcrack jewellery,
your ancient silks,
believing everything I said.

Retreat

Looking back, I see how strange it was;
you drifting from room to room, getting things straight,
modestly winsome in one of last year's dresses;
me with my loveless plans.
It seemed that we would never intercept each other
in that round of flawless summer nights.

Five Winter Poems

You tilt your glass, watching the liquid tense
along the rim, then let the gesture fade.

The moment sours. As I look up
ready to break the silence,

tears surprise you; your lifted hand
is there to ward me off.

Already snow has filled
half the window. Moisture beads the sill.

2

At five the light goes. Shivering,
you turn to me and raise your head
wanting no more than that
sign of tenderness I'm bound to make.

We are too good at this.
Poised on the edge
of the right moment, we both hold back.
Our smiles freeze over.

3

The saloon-bar drunks look ill
under the orange neon.
Weak with laughter,
they gun the engines of lethal cars
and peer into the fog.

Unspeaking, we run the gauntlet
of their exhausts,
not knowing when to stop.
The white fume of our breath
drifts through the freezing air.

4

The countryside is stripped down
ready for real hardship.
Beyond the trim, roadside gardens
night-birds hunt the dark.

You too, in your way,
are fond of this bleakness:
a landscape dull and tough as iron,
the hard face of love.

5

Nothing wears you down
like these chance meetings.
Matching my stride, you look
straight ahead and wait for me to speak.
A wind keens in the high wires.
The season deepens.

Ex Voto

The store is packed with young mothers
confident about bargains.

You are as tireless
as any of them, pacing the narrow aisles

with the air of someone on home ground.
Under your thumb, the meat

spreads its fibres; colour floods
creases in the cellophane.

Smiling, you hold it up until I nod
approval, and the choice is made.

Wrapped and priced, it nestles in your bag,
a good buy hemmed with its own fat.

Frau

Dreaming only of escape,
you spend your mornings at the window
waiting for the first good frost
to go to work on all this lushness.

Nothing stirs as the day lengthens.
All around, the greens
and yellows grow richer, and fatten.

Pulling Out

The place is anybody's now;
its rooms echo as we step into them,
cautious as fugitives.
At this time of day, at this time of the year,
we know what to expect:
flocks of starlings whirring low
over the long meadows,
the outside brickwork warm to our palms,
a light breeze tilting the leaves
as we move along the mud ruts, over the caked grass
for the last time,
our backs to the phalanx of trees
that overlooked our lives for all those years;
and the village quieter now than I ever remember it.
I must have watched this landscape change
more than twenty times.
It never really gives up much of its softness.

Beachcomber

Early July, the light
flexing along the faint
margin where the horizon dipped away—
a pale meniscus. All day long
gulls haunted the shoreline,
flying low. You tired so easily.

Evenings, you roamed
our immaculate rooms,
looking for somewhere to settle;
or I would find you
far out on some slick headland
searching for good pebbles.

That year you had begun to grow your hair.
When you swam it blossomed
blackly, underwater;
then you would let it dry out, in the sun.

On cooler days you walked between
the sea's lip and the crab-pools,
sheathed in your long coat.

Haircut

I sit on a kitchen stool as you clip my hair,
your fingers deft and steady—unconcerned.
The house is quiet,
the children's dreams are good tonight.
We have learned to pretend that we live like this.

Zoological Museum

The snow fox is snarling behind glass,
gums smoothly pink, fangs arched.

Above my head, an osprey is strung out

in full flight. Its wing-tips blur
to bright reflections of the neon strip.

Last night, you were somewhere between

me and the dulled horizon. I drove through
flickerings of moths, thinking how we

have spent our lives

these eight years. You'd waited up:
not drinking, but the room was foul

with cigarette smoke; and you slept

wrapped in a coat, your face, amid the fur,
fragile, as if you wouldn't last the night.

Out

The light craft had been buzzing past all day,
low in the water and built for speed.
From the crown of the fourteenth bridge
the views were endless.
Blue infinities where everything gave way.

She guessed there were risks in small indulgences,
even so, she was glad to be out.
The water pouring back beneath her feet,
the child beginning to move,
everything at blood heat.

Love Game

Dreams took him back,
in which her eyes snagged his;
that look had winded him each time.

Deep in the country
the trains rolled past his room.
Each morning there was cloud-rack, steady rain
blown misty on the high ground.
Each evening blue light flared behind the curtain.

It was a pause: enough to picture her
astray in the sun-bleached contours
of landscapes she had improvised all winter.

The Late Late Show

Near midnight she surfaced
letting her head clear slowly.

The room
focused in on her.

A cowbell on a nail,
bookshelves above the bed,

her antique blouse
crumpled on the cushions.

In a corner, Cybulski bled
through someone's spotless laundry.

Anchorage

Eyes closed, she let show
flecks of scars along one lid.

Small flaws; she treasured them.

Day by day, such things
grew more familiar:

the blue lampshade, off-centre,

neighbours overhead, a virtuoso pianist
in a farther room.

Wizardry

A torrent of neon
floods the street at midnight.

We are miles above it,
working the high wire.

Day Out

It took them hours,
getting through the park.

Blues and crimsons
swam into each other,

the mysteries of order
slowed them down.

He turned with something to say;
a peony

came floating into vision
like an eye-mote.

As if it were a game,
they tended their responses carefully,

disturbing nothing
as their plans came right.

Acid Landscapes

The girl is sitting by an open door
on the first warm day in summer,
wearing a blue fringed shawl
and smoking cigarettes without a pause.

Weeks of rain have left the countryside
tropical, the trailing hedges,
the summer underbrush,
flaccid with growth.

For hours, the sky stays flawless.
A kestrel stoops
to waft a field's length above the sheen
of blown grass;

children come in pairs
down a footpath leading from the beechwood,
looking tired
and talking of themselves.

The girl's adrift
in sunlight, cigarette smoke, and a dream
of those harsh, Northern
acid landscapes:

close-cropped turf
littered with droppings, hillsides chopped
for peat showing their wounds,
crofts rooted in moss.

The wind can soften nothing.
Seaward rocks
lean like figureheads into the rain
that sculpts them to a knife-edge;

lakes are pink
and bitter, yielding fish
scoured like new tin; their glittering
sharpens the mind's eye.

Where she sits
three counties merge. The borders swamp with colour.
She moves beyond the mauve blur of the skyline
to scarps of flint and lichen,

to horizons
clean as a scar on glass,
to muted greens
wrapping the granite closer than a pelt.

A place like that
hones love to brilliance.
She dreams how lovers might
suffer the fierce light flensing their lives

of all but one bald fact;
how they might lie awake by those blunt hills,
breathing each other's breath
and feeling the island slipping with the tides.

Anatomies

Inch by inch, she overhauls his skin,
trailing delicate hands to make the muscles run.

She licks his fingers where the quick is bitten
or presses to make a blemish whiten.

First light is the time they think most about death,
the insights of fatigue luring them both.

Tracking a scar, she sees how skin can wither.
The bruise-marks on her forearms leak into one another.

Fortune

The floor
is littered with coins
cast to tell our future.

Your first words
as we draw apart
might startle the unborn.

Switchblade

The solemn anaemics
are filing out of concert halls,
the final crescendo
seething on their lips.

Life on the streets
defeats them utterly.
They stare out
from the solitude of taxis.

Four stories up
we watch the late drifters,
the renegade guests,
the marriages in abeyance.

You roll the knife
across your dry palm, once.
It flickers open, gleaming
like the promise of another world.

Leap Off the City Skyline

The first step
brought his face up to the sun.

Turning, he fell
through a hall of mirrors

where his eyelids silvered over
and the glow

ran on his face
like highlights on the sea.

That moment gave his purest breath,
sealing his lungs.

That moment
was his last glimpse of the sky:

a fractured blue, and clouds
like dark pools where his other lives submerged.